THE USBORNE BOOK OF
COUNTRIES
OF THE WORLD
FACTS

Neil Champion

CONTENTS

Designed by Stephen Meir, Joe Coonan,
Anil Dumasia and Tony Gibson

Illustrated by Tony Gibson
Additional illustrations by Mario Saporito,
Ian Jackson and Chris Lyon

Researched by Margaret Harvey

Country facts

The 5 largest countries
(square kilometres)

USSR	22,402,000
Canada	9,976,000
China	9,597,000
USA	9,363,000
Brazil	8,512,000

The 5 smallest countries
(square kilometres)

Vatican City	0.4
Monaco	2
Nauru	21
Tuvalu	26
San Marino	61

The largest island

Greenland is the largest island. It is almost 10 times larger than Britain but only 50,000 people live there. This means that if all the people were spread out evenly, each one would have 10,000 times as much room as each person living in Britain.

Longest coastline

Canada has a very jagged coastline 250,000 km (155,000 miles) long. If straightened out it would stretch around the world over 6 times.

Oldest and newest

The oldest country is Iran (or Persia as it used to be known). It has been an independent country since the 6th century BC. The newest country is Brunei, which became independent of Britain in 1984.

The biggest desert

The world's largest desert is the Sahara. It covers part or all of 10 northern and west African countries, including Chad, Niger, Libya, Algeria, Egypt, Mali and Mauritania. It is larger than Australia, the world's sixth largest country. A person left in the desert with no water or shade would die in a day. The temperature can reach 50°C (122°F).

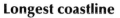

DID YOU KNOW?

The Vatican City, the smallest country in the world, has a population the size of a small village – 1,000 people. One hundred of these are Swiss Guards; their uniforms were designed by Michelangelo in the 15th century.

Amazing But True

Antarctica contains 70 per cent of the world's fresh water in the form of ice. In 1958 one iceberg was spotted that was thought to be the size of Belgium. Antarctica has large deposits of minerals, oil and natural gas, but it is not officially owned by any country.

The largest lake

Lake Superior in Canada is the largest lake in the world. If it were drained of all its water, the land reclaimed would cover an area twice the size of the Netherlands.

Mixed country

Yugoslavia has 2 alphabets (Roman and Cyrillic), 3 religions (Roman Catholic, Eastern Orthodox and Islamic), 4 languages (Macedonian, Serb, Croat, and Slovene), 5 nationalities and 6 republics.

Without a coast

There are 26 countries in the world that do not have a coastline. Switzerland is one of these, but it has a merchant navy.

Busy frontier

More than 120 million people cross the border between Mexico and the USA every year, making it the busiest frontier. The least busy frontier is between East and West Germany, called the Berlin Wall, where only about 200 people cross each year.

DID YOU KNOW?

China has the greatest number of frontiers. It rubs shoulders with 13 other countries.

N. Korea	1.	Laos	10.
USSR	2. 2a.	Vietnam	11.
Mongolia	3.	Macau	12.
Afghanistan	4.	Hong Kong	13.
Pakistan	5.		
India	6. 6a. 6b.		
Nepal	7.		
Bhutan	8.		
Burma	9.		

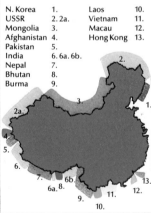

How many countries?

There are now 171 independent countries, whereas in 1900 there were only 53. There are also 56 territories, which were once countries but are not now independent.

Country of islands

Indonesia is made up of over 13,000 islands, together covering about 2 million sq km (770,000 sq miles). This is equal to the area of Mexico.

3

Populations

Largest populations

China	1,042,000,000
India	762,000,000
USSR	278,000,000
USA	239,000,000
Indonesia	170,000,000

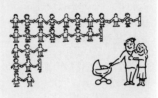

Age distribution

In Africa almost half the population is under 15 years old and only 3 out of 100 can expect to live to 65. In Europe the opposite is true. Only one fifth of the population is under 15 and 12 in every 100 live to be 65.

Population density

Although Australia has a population 3 times larger than Hong Kong, it is 8,000 times larger in area. If the people were spread out evenly over the land each Australian would have 500,000 sq m compared with only 200 sq metres for each person in Hong Kong.

DID YOU KNOW?

The population of New York, the largest city in the USA, is only about 3 per cent of the entire population. But 20 per cent, or 1 in 5, Mexicans live in their biggest city, Mexico City.

Life expectations

Men and women live to an average age of 77 years in Iceland and to an average age of 76 in both Sweden and Japan. In North Yemen and Ethiopia people can expect to live about 40 years.

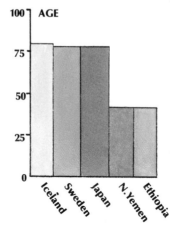

Crowded countries
(people per sq km)

Monaco	17,500
Singapore	4,475
Vatican City	2,500
Malta	1,266
Bangladesh	705
Barbados	650
Bahrain	643
Maldives	536
Mauritius	536
Taiwan	528

More men or women?

For every agricultural worker in Belgium there are at least 10 industrial workers. In Portugal there are almost as many people working on the land as there are in industry.

There are about 20 million more women than men living in Russia. This works out to a ratio of 7 women for every 6 men. But worldwide there are slightly more men than women.

Where no-one is born

In the Vatican City no one is born. This is because married people do not live there. It has a population that remains around 1,000. Kenya, on the other hand, has one of the highest recorded birth rates, with a 5 per cent annual increase in population. This is over twice the worldwide average.

Religions of the world

Christianity is the largest religion, with one fifth of the world belonging to it. Islam (Muslim) is the second largest, with 600 million worshippers (just over half the number of Christians).

Amazing But True

The world population in 1986 is about 5,000 million. It is increasing by 216,000 daily, which means that 150 babies are born a minute. At this rate the world's population will have doubled by 2100 AD.

The emptiest countries
(people per sq km)

Western Sahara	0.5
Mongolia	1.2
Botswana	1.8
Mauritania	1.8
Australia	2.1
Iceland	2.2
Libya	2.3
Canada	2.5
Surinam	2.5
Gabon	3.7

Amazing But True

Honduras will double its population at its present rate of increase by the year AD 2005. East Germany will take until AD 2850 to do the same.

Rich and poor countries

World incomes

Half the population of the world earns a mere 5 per cent of the world's total wealth. A very rich 15 per cent takes two thirds of this wealth.

The poorest people?

By Western standards the Tasaday tribe, who live in the Philippines, are one of the poorest people in the world. They live in caves and do not keep any animals, do not grow crops, make pots or clothes or even use wheels.

How many doctors? (people per doctor)

Top 5 countries		Bottom 5 countries	
USSR	267		
Israel	376	Ethiopia	72,582
Hungary	390	Burkina Faso	55,858
Austria	436	Malawi	47,638
United Arab		Burundi	45,430
Emirates	878	Niger	37,238

How many people can read and write?
(per 1,000 people)

Top 5 countries

Australia	999
USSR	995
France	990
Barbados	990
Canada	980

Bottom 5 countries

Niger	80
Ethiopia	100
Benin	110
Afghanistan	120
N. Yemen	130

DID YOU KNOW?

In the USSR there is on average one hospital bed for every 100 people (about 2½ million beds in all). In Nigeria there is one bed for every 2,500 people (35,000 beds in the country).

Electricity at home

In developed countries most homes have electricity. In poorer countries many families do not. Only 3 per cent of the homes in Haiti, 18 per cent in Paraguay and Pakistan and 25 per cent in Thailand have electricity.

Pakistan

Thailand

Haiti

Paraguay

Water in our homes

In many parts of the world only a few people are lucky enough to have piped water in their homes. In countries like Afghanistan, Ethiopia and Nepal less than one in 10 homes do.

Countries in debt

Many countries have to borrow money from world banks. These have the biggest debts:

Brazil	$102 billion*
Mexico	$95 billion
Argentina	$45 billion
Venezuela	$36 billion
Indonesia	$30 billion

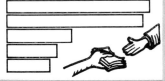

Amazing But True

The 400 richest citizens of the USA have a combined wealth of $118* billion. One saw his fortune increase by $1 billion in a year. This is 12½ million times the average annual wage of a person in Bhutan.

Privately owned cars (cars per 1,000 people)

Top 5 countries		Bottom 5 countries	
USA	499	Bangladesh	0.4
New Zealand	390	Burma	1.2
Canada	389	India	1.2
Australia	368	Burundi	1.3
Luxembourg	365	Chad	1.5

Rich and poor countries

(To find out the average annual income for people in different countries, we have taken the wealth a country makes in a year and divided it evenly between the people who live there.)

Qatar	£22,350*
United Arab Emirates	£20,000
Switzerland	£14,000
USA	£10,000
Malawi	£170
Burma	£150
Bhutan	£130
Bangladesh	£110

*See page 48

Natural products

Top 5 wool producers
(tonnes per year)

Australia	722,000
USSR	460,000
New Zealand	363,000
China	205,000
Argentina	155,000

Most important fibre

Cotton is the world's most important fibre. It was made into cloth over 3,000 years ago in India and Central America. Today it is used to make lace, clothes, sheets, carpets, and industrial products such as thread, film, plastics and special paper.

Amazing But True

The Dutch grow and sell about 3,000 million flowers a year. This is 80,000 flowers for every sq km in the country.

Most expensive oil

The most expensive oil used in perfumes is Musk oil. It sells at $633* for 28 gms or 1 oz. It comes from glands of the male Musk deer, which are found in the mountains of Korea and Mongolia.

Fastest growing plant

Bamboo, used for making window blinds, furniture, floor mats and poles, is one of the fastest growing plants. It can shoot up 90 cms (36 ins) in a day and reaches a height of around 30 m (100 ft). It grows in India, the Far East and China.

Top 5 cotton producers
(tonnes per year)

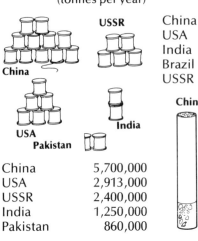

China	5,700,000
USA	2,913,000
USSR	2,400,000
India	1,250,000
Pakistan	860,000

Top 5 tobacco producers
(tonnes per year)

China	1,523,000
USA	640,000
India	594,000
Brazil	400,000
USSR	350,000

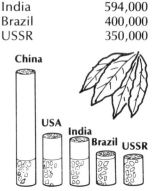

8

*See page 48

Expensive spice

One of the most expensive spices is saffron. It comes from a crocus flower and is used to colour and give an aroma to rice dishes. Grown in China, France, Spain and Iran, over 200,000 stamens are needed to make ½ kilo (1 lb).

The secret of silk

Silk comes from the cocoon of the silkworm. One cocoon contains about a kilometre of thread. It came originally from China, where for hundreds of years its source was kept a secret. One story tells us that in 140 BC a Chinese princess hid some eggs of the silkworm in her hair and took them to Turkestan. From there silk was brought to Europe.

Top 5 rubber producers
(tonnes per year)

Malaysia	1,625,000
Indonesia	1,100,000
Thailand	650,000
India	185,000
Sri Lanka	140,000

Amazing But True

Wild ginseng roots, found in China and Korea, sell for £10,000*for 28 gms (1 oz).

DID YOU KNOW?

Tobacco was first smoked by the American Indians. It was brought to Europe in the 16th century as an ornamental plant. The habit of smoking the dried leaves did not catch on until some years later.

Where rubber comes from

Rubber comes from the sap (called latex) of the rubber tree. To drain it out, the bark has to be cut. Long before Europeans explored the jungles of Central and South America (the original home of the rubber tree) Indians were using latex to waterproof their clothes and footwear.

Best quality wool

Merino wool comes from a breed of sheep that was originally found in Spain. It is considered the best quality wool.

Fuel and energy

Top 10 coal producers
(millions of tonnes per year)

China	763	India	136
USA	751	Australia	125
USSR	485	W. Germany	85
Poland	192	Britain	51
South Africa	140	Czechoslovakia	27

DID YOU KNOW?

More than one third of the world's population still depends on wood for fuel. In some areas of Africa and Asia, timber provides 80 per cent of energy needs. This is equivalent to the use developed nations make of gas and nuclear power.

Fuel consumption

An average American uses about 1,000 times as much fuel in his or her life as does an average Nepalese citizen and about twice as much as a European.

World's largest oil platform

The largest oil platform is the Statfjord B, built at Stavanger in Norway. It weighs 816,000 tonnes, cost £1.1 billion* to construct and needed 8 tugs to tow it into position. It is the heaviest object ever moved in one piece.

Top 10 importers of oil
(millions of tonnes per year)

Japan	183
USA	170
France	70
W. Germany	67
Italy	66
Netherlands	44
Spain	41
Britain	32
Brazil	24
Belgium	18

Nuclear submarines

The first nuclear-powered submarine *(The Nautilus)* was built in the USA in 1955. It travelled 530,000 km (330,000 miles) using only 5 kg (12 lb) of nuclear fuel. A car covering the same distance at an average speed would use 38,000 litres of petrol (8,250 gallons).

Amazing But True

If we could make use of all solar, wind, water and wave power that exists on the earth's surface, we would have 20 billion times as much energy as we need at present.

*See page 48

Longest oil pipeline

The longest oil pipeline stretches from Edmonton, Canada, to Buffalo in New York State, USA. This is a distance of 2,856 km (1,775 miles). If it were laid out like a road, it would take a car 2 days to drive along it doing an average speed of 60 km (38 miles) an hour.

Fuels used in industry since 1850

	1850	1900	1950	2000
Wood	65%	37%	—	—
Coal	10%	55%	59%	—
Oil	—	8%	32%	15%
Gas	—	—	9%	48%
Nuclear	—	—	—	37%

Cause for alarm

By the year AD 2100 some scientists believe that the world could have run out of oil, coal and gas. This may cause some problems as it has also been estimated that we will be using 5½ times as much energy as today.

DID YOU KNOW?

Waterwheels were used in Rome over 2,000 years ago to grind corn. Water power is still used in parts of the world.

Top exporters of oil
(millions of tonnes per year)

Saudi Arabia	168
USSR	129
Britain	79
Iran	78
Mexico	78
United Arab Emirates	60
Nigeria	52
Venezuela	52
Libya	45
Indonesia	41
Iraq	41

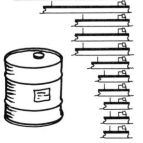

Top 5 producers of uranium (nuclear fuel)
(tonnes per year)

Canada	9,200
USA	7,200
South Africa	5,700
Australia	4,390
Namibia	3,700

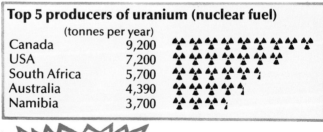

Amazing But True

One tonne of nuclear fuel (uranium) can produce as much energy as 20,000 tonnes of coal. The first nuclear power station was opened in the USSR in 1954.

Metals and precious gems

World's deepest mine

The Western Deep gold mine in South Africa is 3,480 m (12,720 ft) deep. This makes it almost 9 times deeper than the tallest building is high and about 2½ times deeper than the deepest cave. It has a temperature up to 55°C (131°F) at the bottom and is cooled by special refrigerators for people working there.

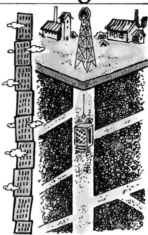

Top 5 copper producer
(tonnes per year)

Chile	1,290,000
USA	1,091,000
USSR	1,020,000
Canada	712,000
Zambia	565,000

Lighter than steel

Aluminium is used to make beer and soft drink cans. A very light metal, it is replacing steel in such things as aircraft, cars, cameras, window-frames and bicycles.

Commonest precious metal

Silver is the commonest precious metal. It is lighter than gold. About half the silver mined is used as a coating for photographic film.

Largest underground mine

The San Manuel Mine in Arizona, USA, is the largest underground mine. This copper mine has over 573 km (350 miles) of tunnels. If laid out in a straight line, the tunnels would reach Los Angeles, California.

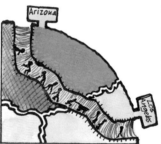

Top 5 tin producers
(tonnes per year)

Malaysia	41,000
Indonesia	23,000
Thailand	21,000
Brazil	20,000
USSR	17,000

Amazing But True

South Africa produces 3 times as much gold each year as its nearest rival, the USSR. It mines 595 million gms (21 million ozs): 28 gms or 1 oz of pure gold can be beaten into a fine wire that would stretch 88 km (55 miles).

Top 10 iron ore miners
(tonnes per year)

USSR	135,000,000
Brazil	61,000,000
China	61,000,000
Australia	57,000,000
USA	35,000,000
India	26,000,000
Canada	25,000,000
South Africa	15,000,000
Liberia	11,000,000
Sweden	11,000,000

Worth its weight

Platinum is the most expensive metal in the world. Unlike silver, it does not tarnish and is used in jewellery for mounting precious gems.

Top 5 lead producers
(tonnes per year)

USA	920,000
USSR	800,000
Japan	362,000
W. Germany	357,000
Britain	338,000

Top 5 aluminium miners
(tonnes per year)

Australia	32,000,000
Guinea	14,700,000
Jamaica	8,700,000
Brazil	6,300,000
USSR	6,200,000

Australia
Guinea
Jamaica
Brazil
USSR

DID YOU KNOW?

The *Cullinan*, once the largest uncut diamond, was discovered in South Africa in 1905. It was the size of a man's fist and weighed over ½ kg (1 lb). The largest gem cut from it, named the 'Star of Africa', is in the British Royal Sceptre in the Tower of London.

The oldest gems

India has records going back to 300 BC that tell us about the mining of moonstones, sapphires, diamonds, emeralds, garnets and agates.

A tough gem

Diamonds are 90 times harder than any other naturally occuring substance. Some are used in industry for cutting very hard substances. Dentists use them on their drills.

DID YOU KNOW?

The world's most valuable gem stone is not the diamond but the ruby. The largest cut stone comes from Burma and weighs 1184 carats (one carat = 200 mgs). It is thought to be worth over $7½ million.*

The golden fleece

Some streams and rivers carry gold particles after running over rocks containing the precious metal. An ancient method of extracting this gold was to put a sheep's fleece in the stream, trapping the tiny pieces of metal in the wool.

City of Jewels

Ratnapura, in Sri Lanka, is known as the 'City of Jewels' because of the amazing variety of gems found there. These include sapphires, diamonds and rubies.

*See page 48

Business and industry

Top 5 car producers
(cars per year)

USA	7,700,000
Japan	7,073,000
W. Germany	3,788,000
France	2,910,000
USSR	1,300,000

DID YOU KNOW?

China makes three times as many bicycles as its closest rivals, the USA and Japan. If the 17½ million made in a year were ridden end to end they would stretch three quarters of the way round the world.

Giant companies

Exxon, a giant oil company in New York, earns more money in a year than many countries. Its sales have reached as high as $90,000 million*, which is about equal to the national income of Belgium.

Stock exchanges

Stock Exchanges are places where governments and companies sell shares and raise money. There are 138 in the world at present, the oldest being in Amsterdam which dates from 1602. The London Stock Exchange alone does over £1,000 million*worth of business a day.

The largest tanker

The *Seawise Giant,* a Japanese supertanker built in 1981, is the largest tanker in the world. It is almost ½ km (a third of a mile) long, equal to about 5 football pitches end to end. It can carry 565,000 tonnes of crude oil around the world. It would take 15 of these supertankers to supply the USA with her daily needs of imported oil, or 5,500 tankers every year.

Most expensive land

Land in the centre of Hong Kong costs £120,000 per sq m (£11,000 per sq ft) to rent. Even a small company could expect to pay up to £1 million*per year for floor space.

Who makes the most?
(amount produced per year)

Typewriters	Japan	2,998,000
Refrigerators	USSR	5,933,000
Socks	USSR	976,000,000
Calculators	Japan	52,435,000
Pianos	Japan	360,338

14

*See page 48

The power of oil

Over 30 countries in the world make money from exporting only one thing – oil. The biggest producers are Saudi Arabia, USSR, United Arab Emirates and Nigeria. Saudi Arabia alone has one third of world output. Oil accounts for one quarter of world trade.

Top 5 radio producers
(radios per year)

Hong Kong	47,986,000
China	19,990,000
Singapore	15,165,000
Japan	13,338,000
USA	11,089,000

Top 5 TV producers
(sets per year)

Japan	13,275,000
USA	12,084,000
USSR	8,578,000
South Korea	7,641,000
China	6,840,000

Largest papermill

The Union Camp Corporation at Savannah, USA, is the largest paper mill, producing almost 100,000 tonnes of paper a year. This is equal to about 28,000,000 sheets of A4 paper, or 250,000 paperback books, a day.

The oldest company

The Faversham Oyster Fishery Company, Britain, has been going since before 1189. This makes it the oldest company on record.

Advertising products

The USA spends more money on advertising than all the other countries of the world put together. In 1978,

Amazing But True

Nippon Steel of Tokyo, Japan, produces about 27 million tonnes of steel a year. This is enough to cover all of Spain and Portugal if the steel was beaten out paper-thin.

during the Super Bowl football match final, the price of advertising on American TV was $325,000* a minute.

Farming

Top grain and bean producers
(tonnes per year)

Soya beans	USA	43,969,000
Barley	USSR	54,500,000
Corn (maize)	USA	106,300,000
Wheat	USSR	82,000,000
Rice	China	172,000,000

Top 5 potato growers
(tonnes per year)

USSR	83,000,000
China	50,000,000
Poland	34,551,000
USA	14,742,000
India	10,100,000

Top 5 banana growers
(tonnes per year)

Brazil	6,692,000
Ecuador	2,000,000
Mexico	1,624,000
Colombia	1,280,000
Honduras	1,250,000

A field of wheat

About 750 years ago, an average sized field of wheat may have provided enough food for 5 people for a year. Today, the same field in a developed country would feed between 20 and 50 people for a year and supply enough seed to sow for the next crop.

Largest mixed farms

The world's largest mixed (arable and dairy) farms are in the USSR. Farms of over 25,000 hectares (62,000 acres) are not uncommon. This is over 600 times larger than the world's smallest country, the Vatican City, and twice the size of Malta.

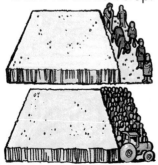

Top 5 beef producers
(tonnes per year)

USA	10,951,000
USSR	7,200,000
Argentina	2,510,000
EEC	2,506,000
Brazil	2,200,000

Top 5 milk producers
(tonnes per year)

USSR	89,600,000
USA	61,553,000
France	34,500,000
W. Germany	25,550,000
UK	16,720,000

A land of sheep

In Australia there are more than 3 times as many sheep as people. The largest sheep station is in South Australia. It is 1,040,000 hectares (2,560,000 acres). This is larger than Cyprus.

Top 5 grape growers
(tonnes per year)

Italy	12,255,000
France	8,550,000
USSR	7,200,000
Spain	5,046,000
USA	4,796,000

Top 5 sugar producers
(tonnes per year)

Brazil	9,200,000
USSR	8,150,000
Cuba	7,800,000
India	6,420,000
China	5,040,000

DID YOU KNOW?

American scientists have predicted that they will be able to breed cows weighing 4.5 tonnes. This is about the size of an elephant.

Experiments with food

What do you get when you cross the American buffalo with an ordinary cow? The beefalo of course! This animal has been bred to produce more meat to help world food production.

Bacteria Pizza with chips

BACTERIA SAUCE

Bacteria Burger

Chef's special Triple decker Bacteria Sandwich

Amazing But True

A certain type of bacteria grown on petrol can be used as a source of food. The bacteria multiplies at a rate of 32,000,000 a day. It is harvested and processed into a highly nutritious food.

Top 5 butter producers
(tonnes per year)

USSR	1,290,000
India	730,000
France	600,000
USA	595,000
W. Germany	530,000

Forestry

Top 5 softwood producers
(cubic metres per year)

USSR	86,000,000
USA	54,000,000
Canada	38,000,000
Japan	30,000,000
Sweden	10,000,000

Top 5 hardwood producers
(cubic metres per year)

USA	17,000,000
USSR	12,000,000
China	8,000,000
Japan	7,000,000
Malaysia	5,000,000

The tallest tree

The largest living thing on earth is the giant redwood tree, growing in the USA and Canada. The tallest is 112 m (367 ft) high. This is considerably taller than the Statue of Liberty, New York, which stands at 93 m (305 ft).

DID YOU KNOW?

The fastest growing tree in the world is the Eucalyptus. One tree in New Guinea grew 10.5 m (35 ft) in 1 year. This is almost 3 cm (over 1 in) a day. In contrast, a Sika Spruce inside the Arctic Circle takes some 98 years to grow 28 cm (11 in); some 4,000 times slower.

Forests in peril

Nearly half the world's rain forests have been cut down and are still being cut down at a rate of 24 sq km (9 sq miles) an hour or 200,000 sq km (80,000 sq miles) a year – an area almost the size of Britain.

The rubber tree

Rubber trees were originally found only in the Amazon rain forest. In 1876 Sir Henry Wickham shipped 70,000 seeds to Kew Gardens in London. Seedlings were then sent to Sri Lanka and Malaysia where rubber plantations were started.

The oldest tree

Some bristlecone pines found in California, USA, are over 4,500 years old.

The lightest wood

Wood from the Balsa tree weighs 40 kg per cubic metre (2½ lb per cubic ft). It is the world's lightest wood. The black ironwood tree is forty times heavier.

Top 5 producers of paper
(tonnes per year)

USA	54,117,000
Japan	15,880,000
W. Germany	7,619,000
China	5,745,000
France	5,041,000

World's largest forest

About 25 per cent of the world's forests cover an area of the northern USSR and Scandinavia up to the Arctic Circle. It is the world's largest forest.

A tree of gold

In 1959 a nursery in the USA bought a single Golden Delicious apple tree for $51,000 (at the time, £18,214)*, making it the most expensive tree the world has known.

Amazing But True

A fire raged non-stop for 10 months from September 1982 in Borneo. It spread over 36,000 sq km (22,000 sq miles). In all, about 13,500 sq km (8,000 sq miles) of forest was destroyed. Several rare species of trees and wild life were made extinct.

World of trees

There are about 40 million sq km (25,000,000 sq miles) of forest in the world. This is about equal to the area of the 3 largest countries (USSR, Canada and China).

*See page 48

Fishing

Freezer trawlers

Fish caught at sea are often frozen on board the trawlers. They are gutted and left in piles to freeze together. Once back in port, they are defrosted, filleted and sold.

Top fish-eating nation

The Japanese eat their way through 3,400 million kg (7,500 million lbs) of fish a year. This means that each person has an average 30 kg (65 lbs) of fish a year. They are the world's biggest fish-eating nation. Their nearest rivals, the Scandinavians, eat only half as much fish on average and the Americans only one fifth.

Amazing But True

Over 95 per cent of all the fish caught in the world are caught in the Northern Hemisphere.

DID YOU KNOW?

A special substance found in the scales of some fish (especially herrings) is used to make a paint. This paint is coated on to glass beads to make imitation pearls.

The most expensive fish

The Russian sturgeon fetches the highest price of any fish in the world. The eggs of the female sturgeon (caviare) are a prized delicacy. The best caviare costs over £28 for 50 gms (1¾ ozs) or £570 per kg. (£258 per lb).*

Top 5 most caught fish
(millions of tonnes per year)

Alaska Pollack	4.5
Japanese Pilchard	4
Chilean Pilchard	3.25
Atlantic Cod	2.25
Chilean Jack Mackerel	2

Top 3 oyster catchers
(tonnes per year)

Japan	250,288
Korea	189,204
USA	81,336

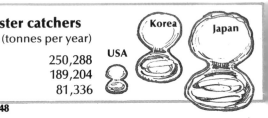

*See page 48

Greatest catch

The most fish ever caught in one haul was made by a Norwegian trawler. It is estimated that in one net it pulled on board more than 120 million fish; over 2,400 tonnes in all. This is enough to feed every man, woman and child in Norway for two weeks.

Fish farming

Many countries now breed fish in special underwater farms. These are the leading countries in this sort of farming:

(in tonnes per year)

China	2,300,000
India	600,000
USSR	300,000
Japan	250,000
Indonesia	240,000

Largest fishing vessel

A whaling factory ship built in the USSR in 1971, called *The Vostok* weighs 26,400 tonnes making it the largest fishing vessel in the world. It is 224.5 m (736.7 ft) long, which means that you could fit 9½ tennis courts end to end along its deck.

Fishing with birds

In Japan, cormorants are trained to catch fish and to fly back to a boat. Each bird is stopped from swallowing the fish by a tight leather collar round its neck.

DID YOU KNOW?

Out of all the fish caught in the world, about three quarters are eaten as food. The other quarter is used to make such things as glue, soap, margarine, pet food and fertilizer.

Amazing But True

A prehistoric fish that was thought to have become extinct about 70 million years ago, was caught in the sea off South Africa. It is called the coelacanth and since 1938 many more of these fish have been caught.

Top 5 fishing countries
(tonnes per year)

Japan	11,800,000
USSR	10,500,000
China	6,193,000
USA	4,741,000
Chile	4,499,000

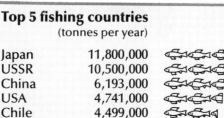

Food and drink

How many calories?

Calories measure the energy content of different foods. We all need a certain amount every day to make our bodies work properly. People in Europe and the USA eat about 3,500 calories a day. Many people in Asia and Africa get at most 2,700. Some people in these countries live on a very poor diet. This may consist of beans, vegetables and grains, and be too low in calories and protein.

Amazing But True

People in Europe and the USA now eat about 20 times as much sugar and at least 5 times as much fat as they did in 1800. This may have something to do with the increase in heart disease in western countries.

Top 5 wine producers
(hectolitres per year)

Italy	75,000,000
France	69,000,000
Spain	42,430,000
USSR	32,248,000
Argentina	23,302,000

A world-wide drink

Top 5 beer producers
(hectolitres per year)

USA	229,000,000
W. Germany	91,000,000
USSR	66,000,000
Britain	60,000,000
Japan	50,000,000

There are 171 countries in the world and Coca-cola is sold in about 157 of them. In one day, sales reached about 280 million cans. This means that if all the cans sold in one month were placed on top of each other they would make three chains each reaching the moon.

DID YOU KNOW?

The largest cake ever was baked in New Jersey, USA, in 1982. It weighed in at 37 tonnes – equal to the weight of 7 elephants.

Meals within meals

Bedouin sometimes prepare a meal of stuffed, roast camel for wedding feasts. They start by stuffing a fish with eggs, putting this inside a chicken, the chicken inside a whole roast sheep and the lot inside a cooked camel.

Most nutritious fruit

The avocado pear contains about 165 calories for every 100 gms of edible fruit. This is more than eggs or milk. It also contains twice as much protein as milk, and more vitamin A, B and C. In contrast, the cucumber has only 16 calories per 100 gms.

Most expensive food

The First Choice Black Perigord truffle, found in France, costs £8.50 for a 12.5 g (½ oz tin) or £680 a kg (£309 per pound).*

Top 5 honey producers
(tonnes per year)

USSR	193,000	
China	115,000	
USA	81,600	
Mexico	62,000	
Argentina	34,000	

Top 5 tea growers
(tonnes per year)

India	565,000	
China	397,000	
Sri Lanka	190,000	
USSR	140,000	
Japan	99,000	

Top 5 coffee producers
(tonnes per year)

Brazil	1,003,000	
Colombia	840,000	
Indonesia	266,000	
Ivory Coast	250,000	
Mexico	234,000	

Super sausage

A sausage-maker in Birmingham, Britain, made one specimen that was 9 km (5½ miles) long. This amounts to about 87,000 ordinary sausages.

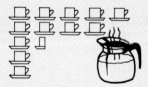

*See page 48

A monster melon

The largest melon weighed over 90 kg (14 stone). The size of a large human being, it would have fed 400 people.

Buildings and structures

The largest hotel

It would take more than 8½ years for one person to sleep in every room of the Hotel Rossiya, Moscow. The 3,200 rooms can put up 5,350 guests. There are 93 lifts and about 3,000 staff.

DID YOU KNOW?

The most expensive hotel in the world is the Hotel Nova Park in Elysées in Paris, France. The Royale Suite costs £3,525* a night. This is more than many French people earn in a year.

World's longest wall

The Great Wall of China stretches for 3,460 km (2,150 miles), ranges between 4½ and 12 m (15 and 40 ft) high, and is up to 10 m (32 ft) thick. Another 2,860 km (1,780 miles) can be added because of spurs and kinks. This makes it as long as the River Nile, the longest river in the world. Six Great Walls laid end to end would reach round the circumference of the Earth.

The largest palace

The Imperial Palace in the centre of Beijing, China, covers an area of 72 hectares (178 acres). This is equal to 100 football pitches. It is surrounded by the largest moat in the world – 38 km (23½ miles) in length.

The tallest buildings

Sears Tower, Chicago, USA	443 metres
World Trade Center, New York, USA	411 metres
Empire State Building, New York, USA	381 metres
Standard Oil Building, Chicago, USA	346 metres
John Hancock Center, Chicago, USA	343 metres
Chrysler Building, New York, USA	319 metres
Bank of China, Hong Kong	315 metres
60 Wall Tower, New York, USA	290 metres
First Canadian Place, Toronto, Canada	289 metres
40 Wall Tower, New York, USA	282 metres

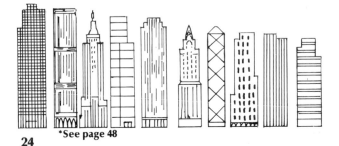

Highest homes

The highest settlement is on the Indian and Tibetan border. Basisi is 5,988 m (19,650 ft) above sea level. This is only 2,860 m (9,384 ft) lower than Mount Everest, the highest mountain in the world.

*See page 48

The highest dam

The highest dam is in Switzerland. The Grande Dixence is 285 m (935 ft) from the base to the rim and cost a staggering £151 million*in 1961 when it was completed. This is only 15 m (50 ft) short of the Eiffel Tower in Paris.

The oldest buildings

Twenty-one huts were discovered in 1960 in Nice, France, that have been dated to 400,000 BC. They are the oldest recognizable buildings in the world.

Smallest house

A fisherman's cottage in North Wales has only 2 tiny rooms and a staircase inside. The outside measures 1.8 m (6 ft) wide and only just over 3 m (10 ft) high.

DID YOU KNOW?

The longest bridge span in the world is the Humber Estuary Bridge, Britain. It is 1,410 m (4,626 ft) across. It was opened in 1981, having taken 9 years to build.

The tallest lighthouse

The steel tower lighthouse in Yokohama, Japan, is 106 m (348 ft) high. But almost 7 of these would be needed standing on top of each other to reach the world's tallest structure, the Warszawa Radio Mast in Poland.

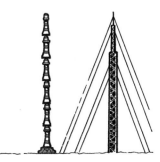

Seven Wonders

The Seven Wonders of the World were first mentioned in the 2nd century BC by a man called Antipater of Sidon. They were:

The Pyramids of Giza, Egypt
The Hanging Gardens of Babylon, Iraq
The Tomb of King Mausolus, Turkey
The Temple of Diana, Ephesus, Turkey
The Colossus of Rhodes, Greece
The Statue of Jupiter, Olympia, Greece
The Pharos of Alexandria, Egypt

Of the Seven Wonders, only the pyramids are still standing. The others have been destroyed by fire, earthquake and invading nations.

*See page 48

Cities

Fastest growing city

Mexico City is at present growing at a rate of 25 per cent every 5 years. With a population of 16 million it is estimated that by the year 2000, it will be over 31 million. This is 5 times as many people as there are in all Switzerland at present.

The largest town

Mount Isa, Queensland, Australia, spreads over almost 41,000 sq km (15,800 sq miles). It covers an area 26 times greater than that of London and is about the same size as Switzerland.

Top 10 most crowded cities
(people per city)

Mexico City	16,000,000
Sao Paulo	12,600,000
Shanghai	11,900,000
Tokyo	11,600,000
Buenos Aires	9,700,000
Beijing	9,200,000
Calcutta	9,200,000
New York	9,100,000
Rio de Janeiro	9,000,000
Paris	8,500,000

Traffic City

The greatest amount of vehicles in any city is to be found in Los Angeles, USA. At one interchange almost 500,000 vehicles were counted in a 24-hour period during a weekday. This is an average of 20,000 cars and trucks an hour.

The cheapest city

In 1626 a Dutchman bought an island in America from some local Indians. He gave them some cloth and beads worth about $24 for an area of land he thought covered 86 sq km (34 sq miles). In fact it was 57 sq km (22 sq miles). But it was still a bargain. He had bought Manhattan, now one of the most crowded and expensive islands in the world. He named his town New Amsterdam but it was later renamed New York.

How many people live in cities?

About one third of people in the world live in towns or cities. By the year 2000, experts believe that over half will live in urban areas. But this may vary from place to place. In the USA about 74 per cent live in towns and cities compared with 20 per cent in India.

The oldest city

Archaeologists believe that Jericho, in Jordan, is the oldest continuously inhabited place. There were as many as 3,000 people living there as early as 7,800 BC.

Longest underground

London has 400 km (247 miles) of underground tracks, making it the longest in the world. This includes 267 stations and about 450 trains. All the track laid end to end would stretch from London to Land's End in Cornwall.

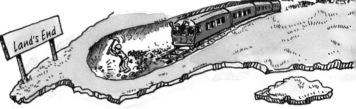

An island city

Venice, in the north of Italy, is built on 118 islands in a lagoon. Canals serve as streets and roads and everybody uses boats instead of cars to get around. There are over 400 bridges crossing the canals.

Poles apart

The most northerly capital is Reykjavik in Iceland. The southern-most is Wellington, New Zealand. They are 20,000 km (12,500 miles) apart.

The longest name

Krung Thep is the shortened name of the capital of Thailand, known in the West as Bangkok. Its full name has 167 letters and means in English,

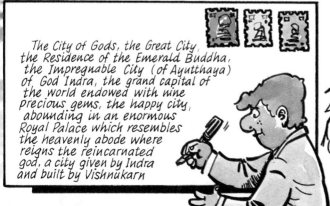

The City of Gods, the Great City, the Residence of the Emerald Buddha, the Impregnable City (of Ayutthaya) of God Indra, the grand capital of the world endowed with nine precious gems, the happy city, abounding in an enormous Royal Palace which resembles the heavenly abode where reigns the reincarnated god, a city given by Indra and built by Vishnukarn

So far from the sea

Urungi, capital of the Uighur Autonomous Region in China, is the furthest city from the sea. It is about 2,250 km (1,400 miles) from the nearest coast.

Communications

Telephones – top 5 countries
(per 1,000 people)

Monaco	1,071
Sweden	828
USA	788
Switzerland	741
Canada	670

Televisions – top 5 countries
(per 1,000 people)

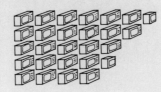

Monaco	654
USA	624
Japan	537
Canada	476
Italy	390

Largest and smallest book

The smallest published book measures 1.4 x 1.4 mm. Only 200 copies were printed in Tokyo, Japan. The book is a children's story called *Ari (The Ant)*. Over 4 million copies would fit on the cover of the world's largest book (the *Super Book*), which measures 2.74 x 3.07 m (9 x 10 ft).

Secret codes

Coded messages have been used since 400 BC. Probably the best known is the Morse code, invented in the 19th century by Samuel Morse.

Newspapers – top 10 countries
(bought daily per 1,000 people)

Japan	575
Liechtenstein	558
E. Germany	530
Sweden	524
Finland	515
Norway	483
Britain	421
Iceland	420
Monaco	410
W. Germany	408

Dates of famous inventions

Telephone	1876
Gramophone	1877
Moving film	1885
Television	1934
Audio film	1927
Tape recorder	1935
Photocopier	1938
Computer	1946
Transistor radio	1948
Stereo recording	1958
Microcomputer	1969

Amazing But True

A black and white TV with a 3.5 cm (1⅖ in) screen was designed and made by Seiko in Japan. It fits on to a wrist watch. The smallest colour TV has a 21 cm (8 in) screen.

Longest telephone cable

A telephone cable running beneath the Pacific Ocean links Canada and Australia via New Zealand and the Hawaiian Islands. It is 14,500 km (9,000 miles) long and cost £35 million* in 1963 to build.

Crossed wires

The Pentagon, Washington DC, is the centre of American defence. It has the largest switchboard in the world. About 25,000 telephone lines can be used at the same time.

*See page 48

Mail bag

The USA has the largest postal service in the world. In one year its citizens sent over 120 billion letters and packages. This is equal to 521 letters a year or about 1½ letters a day, for everyone living in America.

Communicating flags

Semaphore is a method of signalling with flags. With one flag in each hand, the signaller holds them in different positions to spell out the alphabet. A way of passing messages over a short distance, it was invented by the French army in 1792 during the French Revolution.

Computers for the disabled

The *Sprite* is a piece of computer technology that has been designed to imitate the human voice. It helps those with speech problems.

A long-distance chat

Men have talked to each other directly between the moon and the earth, a distance of 400,000 km (250,000 miles), making this the longest distance chat. A powerful radio signal sent into space is expected to take 24,000 years to reach its destination, a group of stars 10 billion times further away than the moon. It could be the longest awaited reply.

A golden pen

The ballpoint pen was invented in 1938 by a Hungarian named Biro. In its first year in the UK 53 million were sold.

Newspaper facts

When *The Times* newspaper reported Nelson's victory over the French at the Battle of Trafalgar in 1805, the news took 2½ weeks to reach London. When the same newspaper, 164 years later, showed pictures of the first men on the moon, they came out only a few hours after the landing.

DID YOU KNOW?

The world's first postage stamp was the *Penny Black,* issued in Britain in May, 1840. A one-cent British Guiana stamp of 1856, of which there is only one known example, is thought to be worth £500,000.*

Shrinking world

Using satellites orbiting the earth, television can now reach a potential audience of about 2½ billion people. An event like the Olympic Games, can be beamed live into the homes of half the people in the world.

Travel

Airship travel

Hydrogen-filled airships were in regular use up until 1938, taking people across the Atlantic. They were stopped because too many caught on fire.

Road building

To move their armies the Romans built over 80,000 km (50,000 miles) of road in Europe and the Middle East. After their conquest of Britain, it took only 6 days by horse to get from London to Rome. About 1,500 years later in the 19th century, it took just as long.

Most travelled person

An American, named Jesse Rosdall, went to all the countries and territories in the world except North Korea and the French Antarctic. He claimed to have travelled a total of 2,617,766 km (1,626,605 miles). This is equal to almost 7 trips to the moon or 65 journeys round the world.

Petrol consumption

In the USA over 1,400 million litres (300 million gallons) of petrol a day are used. This is enough petrol in a year to fill an oil drum 36.5 km (22.6 miles) high and 26.5 km (16.5 miles) wide. A total of over 20,000 km^3, it would fill Lake Baykal in the USSR, the lake with the greatest volume.

Top 5 road countries
(kilometres of road)

USA	6,365,590
Canada	3,002,000
France	1,502,000
Brazil	1,411,936
USSR	1,408,800

Longest and shortest flight

The shortest scheduled flight (from the island of Westray to Papa Westray off Scotland, lasting 2 minutes) could be made over 450 times while one jet makes a non-stop journey from Sydney to San Francisco, a total of 7,475 km (4,645 miles).

The first car

The first petrol-driven car took to the roads in 1885. It had 3 wheels and a tiller to steer. Its top speed was 16 kph (10 mph). Just 100 years later there are enough vehicles in the world for every tenth person to own one. If they all met in one traffic jam, it would go round the world 34 times.

DID YOU KNOW?

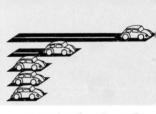

Concorde travels faster than the speed of sound, cruising at 2,333 kph (1,500 mph). It flies between London and New York in 3 hours, a distance of 5,536 km (3,500 miles). This is over twice as fast as an ordinary passenger plane.

Widest and narrowest

The widest road in the world is the Monumental Axis in Brasilia, Brazil. It is 250 m (820 ft) wide, which is wide enough for 160 cars side by side. It is over 500 times wider than the narrowest street, which is in Port Isaac, Britain. At its narrowest it is a mere 49 cm (1½ ft) and is known as 'squeeze-belly alley'.

World famous train

The Orient Express once ran between Paris and Istanbul. It now makes a shorter trip from London to Venice. It offers the highest luxury in travel. A one-way ticket costs at present £475.* This is also the price of a single airfare to Sydney, Australia, a city 14 times further away from London than Venice.

Busiest rail network

About 18½ million people use trains in Japan every day. If one train carried them all, it would have about 370,000 carriages and would stretch for over 3,300 km (2,000 miles).

Fastest train

A special passenger train (called a TGV) which runs between Paris and Lyons, France, has an average speed of 212.5 kph (132 mph). It reaches 270 kph (168 mph) on its 425 km (264 mile) journey, which takes 2 hours in all.

Top 5 railway countries
(kilometres of track)

USA	288,072
USSR	240,400
Canada	67,066
India	60,933
China	50,000

Amazing But True

The Boeing 747 (Jumbo Jet) is the largest and most powerful plane. It can carry up to 500 passengers. It stands as high as a 6-storey office block and weighs over 370 tonnes. It has a maximum speed of 969 kph (602 mph) and a wing-span of over 70 m (232 ft).

The bicycle

An early form of bicycle, called a hobbyhorse or walk-along, was popular in the mid-17th century. It had no pedals. We had to wait almost 200 years for their invention.

Top holiday countries
(number of visitors)

Italy	48,311,474
Spain	42,011,000
France	33,156,000
USA	23,086,000
Austria	14,253,000
Canada	12,183,000
UK	11,637,000
W. Germany	9,460,000
Switzerland	9,186,000
Hungary	6,473,000

*See page 48

Money*

World's largest mint

The largest mint – the factory where coins are made – is in the USA. It can make 22 million coins a day using almost 100 stamping machines. It covers an area of 4½ hectares (11 acres). At full production it could produce a pile of coins 5 times higher than Mount Everest in just one day.

Earliest coins

Coins found in Lydia (Turkey) date from the reign of King Gyges in the 7th century BC. These coins below were found in Sicily and date to the 5th century BC.

Highest value note

A few, very rare, $10,000* notes exist in America. They are not in general circulation.

*See page 48

Amazing But True

The American ambassador to India handed over in 1974 a cheque for 16,640 million rupees (£852,791,660)* on behalf of his government to the Indian government. It was the largest cheque ever written.

Military spending

The USA spends over $500 billion* on defence in a year which is more than all the people in China, India and Indonesia earn in the same period. The USA and the USSR together spend more on arms than the rest of the world.

Highest paid job

The chairman of the First Boston Corporation, an American-based company, earned $5,215 a day in 1984. This made an annual salary of $2 million (£1,200,000).*

Sunken treasure

Almost 2,000 Spanish galleons lie off the coast of Florida and the Bahamas. They were sunk in the 16th century, most of them carrying large amounts of gold. This area is the largest untapped storehouse of treasure in the world.

Golden Beatle

Paul McCartney, songwriter and ex-Beatle, earns an estimated £25 million a year from his records. This is about £45 a minute or £70,000* a day.

DID YOU KNOW?

The Chinese one kwan note printed in the 14th century was 92.8 x 33 cm (9 x 13 in). It is 73 times larger than the smallest note, the 10 bani issued in Romania in 1917.

Income Tax

Many governments take a certain amount of money from the salaries of their citizens. This is called Income Tax. It was introduced in Britain in 1799 by the Prime Minister, William Pitt. He needed money to pay for the war against Napoleon. The war ended over 150 years ago, but Income Tax has remained.

Different money

Coins and notes are not the only form of money. Teeth of animals, metal bracelets and necklaces, shells, axe heads, knives, blocks of salt and even blocks of tea leaves have been used. The word *cash* comes from an Indian word meaning compressed tea and the word *salary* comes from the Latin word for salt. Both were used to pay people in the past.

Honesty rules

In 1972 $500,000* was found by a man in Lower Elliot, USA. The money was dropped by a criminal escaping by parachute. Resisting the temptation to keep the money, he tracked down the owner and returned every cent.

Powerful banks

The world's most wealthy bank is Citicorp, based in New York. Only the US Government handles more money in a year. The 56 poorest countries each have less wealth than each of the top 500 commercial banks in the world.

Money loses value

When the price of buying things goes up, money becomes worth less. This is called inflation. In Germany after the First World War, the German Mark dropped in value. In 1921, 81 Marks were worth 1 American dollar. Two years later, the same dollar was worth 1 million Marks.

Great Train Robbery

In 1963 over £2½ million* was stolen from a train in Buckinghamshire, England. Only one seventh of the total was ever recovered. It was the costliest train robbery.

33

Languages

10 most spoken languages

Language	Speakers
Chinese	700,000,000
English	400,000,000
Russian	265,000,000
Spanish	240,000,000
Hindustani	230,000,000
Arabic	146,000,000
Portuguese	145,000,000
Bengali	144,000,000
German	119,000,000
Japanese	116,000,000

The first alphabet

The Phoenicians, who once lived where Syria, Jordan and Lebanon are today, had an alphabet of 29 letters as early as 1,700 BC. It was adopted by the Greeks and the Romans. Through the Romans, who went on to conquer most of Europe, it became the alphabet of Western countries.

Sounds strange

One tribe of Mexican Indians hold entire conversations just by whistling. The different pitches provide meaning.

The Rosetta Stone

The Rosetta Stone was found by Napoleon in the sands of Egypt. It dates to about 196 BC. On it is an inscription in hieroglyphics and a translation in Greek. Because scholars knew ancient Greek, they could work out what the Egyptian hieroglyphics meant. From this they learned the language of the ancient Egyptians.

DID YOU KNOW?

Many Chinese cannot understand each other. They have different ways of speaking (called dialects) in different parts of the country. But today in schools all over China, the children are being taught one dialect (Mandarin), so that one day all Chinese will understand each other.

Translating computers

Computers can be used to help people of different nationalities, who do not know each others' language, talk to each other. By giving a computer a message in one language it will translate it into another specified language.

Worldwide language

English is spoken either as a first or second language in at least 45 countries. This is more than any other language. It is the language of international business and scientific conferences and is used by airtraffic controllers worldwide. In all, about one third of the world speaks it.

Earliest writing

Chinese writing has been found on pottery, and even on a tortoise shell, going back 6,000 years. Pictures made the basis for their writing, each picture showing an object or idea. Probably the earliest form of writing came from the Middle East, where Iraq and Iran are now. This region was then ruled by the Sumerians.

Amazing But True

A scientific word describing a process in the human cell is 207,000 letters long. This makes this single word equal in length to a short novel or about 80 typed sheets of A4 paper.

Many tongues

A Frenchman, named Georges Henri Schmidt, is fluent (meaning he reads and writes well) in 31 different languages.

The most words

English has more words in it than any other language. There are about 1 million in all, a third of which are technical terms. Most people only use about 1 per cent of the words available, that is, about 10,000. William Shakespeare is reputed to have made most use of the English vocabulary.

International language

Esperanto was invented in the 1880s by a Pole, Dr Zamenhof. It was hoped that it would become the international language of Europe. It took words from many European countries and has a very easy grammar that can be learned in an hour or two.

The same language

The languages of India and Europe may originally come from just one source. Many words in different languages sound similar. For example, the word for *King* in Latin is *Rex,* in Indian, *Raj,* in Italian *Re,* in French *Roi* and in Spanish *Rey.* The original language has been named Indo-European. Basque, spoken in the French and Spanish Pyrenees, is an exception. It seems to have a different source which is still unknown.

Number of alphabets

There are 65 alphabets in use in the world today. Here are some of them:

Roman
ABCDEFGHIJKLMNOPQRS

Greek
ΑΒΓΔΕΖΗΘΙΚΛΜΝΞΟΠΡ

Russian (Cyrillic)
АЬВГДЕЖЗИЙКЛМНОП

Hebrew
מעדיף כיום דיור בשירות

Chinese
評定。因此我們制定 一種申請房屋計點辦

Arabic
١٨٩٧ وصل إلى إنجلترا أنموذج

Art and entertainment

Most productive painter

Picasso, the Spanish artist who died in 1973, is estimated to have produced over 13,000 paintings, as well as a great many engravings, book illustrations and sculptures, during his long career – he lived to be 91. This means that he painted an average 3½ pictures every week of his adult life.

Most valuable painting

Leonardo da Vinci's *Mona Lisa* is probably the world's most valuable painting. It was stolen from the Louvre, Paris, in 1911, where it had hung since it was painted in 1507. It took 2 years to recover. During that time, 6 forgeries turned up in the USA, each selling for a very high price.

The oldest museum

The Ashmolean Museum in Oxford, Britain, was built in 1679.

The record of records

The *Guinness Book of Records*, first published in 1955, has been translated into 24 languages and has sold over 50 million copies worldwide.

Largest painting

The Battle of Gettysburg, is the size of 10 tennis courts. It took 2½ years to paint (1883) and measures 125 m (410 ft) by 21.1 m (70 ft). The artist was Paul Philippoteaux.

Largest art gallery

The Winter Palace and the Hermitage in Leningrad, USSR, have 322 galleries showing a total of 3 million works of art and archaeological exhibits. A walk around all the galleries is 24 km (15 miles).

Best-selling novelist

Barbara Cartland, a British authoress, has sold about 370 million copies of her romantic novels worldwide and they have been translated into 17 languages. All her books gathered together would make 5,000 piles, each as high as the Eiffel Tower.

Pop records

The Beatles were the most successful pop group of all time. They sold over 1,000 million discs and tapes. The biggest selling single was *White Christmas,* written by Irving Berlin and sung by Bing Crosby. The most successful album is *Thriller* by Michael Jackson, selling over 40 million copies.

Band Aid

On July 13th, 1985, two pop concerts took place, one in Wembley, London, and the other at the JF Kennedy Stadium, Philadelphia. Fifty well-known bands played to raise money for the starving of Africa. By the end of the year over £50 million* had been raised by the concert, a record and a book of the event.

Largest audience

In 1980 the pop star, Elton John, played in front of 400,000 people at a free summer concert in Central Park, New York.

DID YOU KNOW?

The smallest professional theatre in the world is to be found in Hamburg, Germany. *The Piccolo* seats only 30 people. The Perth Entertainment Centre, Australia, has a theatre that holds 80,000, which is a capacity over 2,500 times greater.

William Shakespeare

Shakespeare, commonly thought the world's greatest playwright, wrote 37 plays in all. The longest is *Hamlet.* The role of Hamlet is also the longest written by Shakespeare.

A night at the opera

Richard Wagner had an eccentric patron in Ludwig II, king of Bavaria. He was so impressed by Wagner's music that he built a castle (called Neuschwanstein) in Bavaria for Wagner's operas.

Expensive film

One of the most expensive films ever made was *Star Trek,* which was first shown in 1979. It cost $21 million* to make.

Amazing But True

Wolfgang Amadeus Mozart wrote about 1,000 pieces of music, including many operas and symphonies. He died aged 35, but had been composing since the age of 4. He is thought to be one of the world's greatest composers.

The world of machines

Largest and slowest

The machine that takes the Space Shuttle to its launching pad is called the *Crawler* and for a very good reason. It weighs 3,000 tonnes and travels at a maximum speed of 3 kph (2 mph). It is 40 m (130 ft) long, and 35 m (115 ft) wide.

Oldest working clock

The mechanical clock in Salisbury Cathedral, Britain, dates back to 1386. It is still in full working order, after repairs were made in 1956, some 600 years later.

Earliest steam engine

Richard Trevithick, a Cornish inventor, built the first steam engine in 1803. The first public railway was opened 23 years later between Stockton and Darlington, Britain. The engine used was designed by George Stephenson.

The sewing machine

The sewing machine was first used in France in the early 19th century. It was made of wood. Isaac Singer invented the first foot treadle machine in 1851. This became so popular that it lead to mass-production of sewing machines.

DID YOU KNOW?

The first motorcycle was designed and built by the firm of Michaux-Perreaux in France in 1869. It ran on steam and had a top speed of 16 kph (10 mph). The first petrol-driven motorcycle was designed in 1885 by Gottlieb Daimler. Its top speed was 19 kph (12 mph). Compare this with the 512 kph (318.6 mph) of the fastest modern bike.

Radio fraud

In 1913, almost 50 years after the first radio transmission, an American was convicted of trying to mislead the public. He had advertised that in a few years his radio company would be able to transmit the human voice across the Atlantic to Europe. The district attorney did not believe him. Two years later a trans-Atlantic conversation took place.

A mirror on the universe

The inventor of the telescope is thought to be Roger Bacon, a 13th century monk. His instrument was first discovered in detail in 1608 by a Dutchman. Today, the most powerful telescope is in the USSR. The lens alone is 6 m (19 ft) across and weighs 70 tonnes. It can pick up the light given off from a candle 24,000 km (15,000 miles) away.

Powerful computer

One of the world's most powerful computers, the CYBER Model 205-444 system, can make 800 million calculations a second. If all the people in China could each make a calculation in a second, it would take the entire population to keep up with this computer.

Most powerful fire-engine

A fire-engine designed to tackle aircraft fires can squirt 277 gallons of foam a second out of its 2 turrets. It is the 8-wheeled Oshkosh firetruck. It could fill an olympic-sized swimming pool in only 30 minutes.

Most accurate clock

The Olsen clock in Copenhagen town hall, Denmark, will lose half a second every 300 years. It took 10 years to make. An atomic clock in the USA is accurate to within 1 second in 1,700,000 years.

The fastest official record for typing is 216 words in one minute or 3½ words per second. An electronic printer in the USA can type over 3,000 times faster: that is 700,000 words a minute or 12,000 a second.

The longest cars

In 1927, 6 Bugatti 'Royales' were made in France. They were each 6.7 m (22 ft) long. A custom built Lamrooster measures 15.24 m (50 ft), has 10 wheels and a pool in the back.

World speed records

Steam locomotive	1938	202.77 kph (126 mph)
Helicopter	1978	368.00 kph (228.6 mph)
Motorcycle	1978	512.73 kph (318.6 mph)
Aircraft	1976	3,529.00 kph (2,192.9 mph)
Command Module	1969	39,897 kph (24,791.5 mph)

World map

Alaska

Greenland

Finland

Sweden

Norway

Iceland

Canada

Britain

6

Ireland

2

3

France

10

Portugal

Italy

United States of America

ATLANTIC OCEAN

Spain

Tun

Bermuda

Morocco

Algeria

Lib

Bahamas

Western Sahara

Mexico

Dominican Republic

Cape Verde

Mauritania

Mali

Niger

Cuba

Puerto Rico

Belize

Haiti

Gambia

Senegal

Guatemala

Honduras

Nicaragua

Barbados

Guinea-Bissau

28

Nigeria

El Salvador

Guyana

Guinea

Costa Rica

Venezuela

Surinam

Sierra Leone

Panama

French Guiana

Liberia

Benin

Colombia

Ivory Coast

Togo

32

Gabon

Ghana

PACIFIC OCEAN

Ecuador

Congo

Peru

Brazil

Ang

KEY TO NUMBERS

Bolivia

Paraguay

Nami

Chile

Botswana

1 Denmark
2 West Germany
3 East Germany
4 Poland
5 Czechoslovakia
6 Netherlands
7 Belgium
8 Luxembourg
9 Switzerland
10 Austria
11 Hungary
12 Romania
13 Yugoslavia
14 Bulgaria
15 Albania

South Afri

Uruguay

16 Greece
17 Syria
18 Lebanon
19 Israel
20 Jordan
21 Kuwait
22 Bahrain
23 Qatar
24 United Arab Emirates
25 Bangladesh
26 Kampuchea
27 Singapore

Argentina

Falkland Islands

40

ARCTIC OCEAN

Union of Soviet Socialist Republics

Mongolia

N. Korea

Japan

rkey

China

2

Iraq
Iran

Afghanistan

Bhutan

S. Korea

Pakistan
Nepal

Laos

Taiwan

Saudi
Arabia
Oman

India
Burma

Hong Kong

pt

udan

S Yemen

Vietnam

Philippines

N. Yemen

Djibouti

Thailand

26

Brunei

Ethiopia
Somalia
Maldives
Sri Lanka

Malaysia

Papua New Guinea

Kenya
Seychelles

Indonesia

Solomon
Islands

Tanzania

Comoros

INDIAN OCEAN

Mauritius

Fiji

Reunion
Madagascar

Australia

Mozambique
Swaziland
Lesotho

28 Burkina Faso
29 Chad
30 Cameroon
31 Central African Republic
32 Equatorial Guinea
33 Uganda
34 Rwanda
35 Burundi
36 Malawi
37 Zambia
38 Zimbabwe

New Zealand

41

Countries of the world facts

Country	Capital	Population	Area (sq km)
Afghanistan	Kabul	16,000,000	648,000
Albania	Tirana	2,800,000	29,000
Algeria	Algiers	19,600,000	2,382,000
Andorra	Andorra-la-Vieja	40,000	500
Angola	Luanda	7,800,000	1,247,000
Antigua and Barbuda	St John's	80,000	442
Argentina	Buenos Aires	28,200,000	2,767,000
Australia	Canberra	15,000,000	7,678,000
Austria	Vienna	7,000,000	84,000
Bahamas	Nassau	200,000	14,000
Bahrain	Manama	400,000	600
Bangladesh	Dacca	90,700,000	144,000
Barbados	Bridgetown	300,000	430
Belgium	Brussels	9,900,000	31,000
Belize	Belmopan	160,000	23,000
Benin	Porto Novo	3,600,000	113,000
Bermuda	Hamilton	60,000	50
Bhutan	Thimphu	1,300,000	47,000
Bolivia	La Paz	5,700,000	1,099,000
Botswana	Gaborone	900,000	600,000
Brazil	Brasilia	120,500,000	8,512,000
Brunei	Bandar Seri Begawan	200,000	6,000
Bulgaria	Sofia	8,900,000	111,000
Burkina Faso	Ouagadougou	6,300,000	274,000
Burma	Rangoon	34,100,000	677,000
Burundi	Bujumbura	4,200,000	28,000
Cameroon	Yaoundé	8,700,000	475,000
Canada	Ottawa	24,200,000	9,976,000
Cape Verde	Praia	300,000	4,000
Cayman Islands	Georgetown	20,000	300
Central African Republic	Bangui	2,400,000	623,000
Chad	N'Diamena	4,500,000	1,284,000
Chile	Santiago	11,300,000	757,000
China	Beijing	1,020,000,000	9,597,000
Colombia	Bogota	26,400,000	1,139,000
Comoros	Moroni	400,000	2,000
Congo	Brazzaville	1,700,000	342,000
Costa Rica	San José	2,300,000	51,000
Cuba	Havana	9,700,000	115,000
Cyprus	Nicosia	600,000	9,000
Czechoslovakia	Prague	15,300,000	128,000
Denmark	Copenhagen	5,100,000	43,000
Djibouti	Djibouti	400,000	22,000
Dominica	Roseau	70,000	751
Dominican Republic	Santo Domingo	5,600,000	49,000

Country	Capital	Population	Area (sq km)
Ecuador	Quito	8,600,000	284,000
Egypt	Cairo	43,300,000	1,001,000
El Salvador	San Salvador	4,700,000	21,000
Equatorial Guinea	Malabo	400,000	28,000
Ethiopia	Addis Ababa	31,800,000	1,222,000
Falkland Islands	Stanley	2,000	12,000
Fiji	Suva	600,000	18,000
Finland	Helsinki	4,800,000	337,000
France	Paris	55,000,000	551,000
French Guiana	Cayenne	60,000	91,000
Gabon	Libreville	700,000	268,000
Gambia	Banjul	600,000	11,000
Germany, East	Berlin	16,700,000	108,000
Germany, West	Bonn	61,700,000	249,000
Ghana	Accra	11,800,000	239,000
Greece	Athens	9,700,000	132,000
Greenland	Godthaab	50,000	2,186,000
Grenada	St George's	100,000	344
Guadeloupe	Basse-Terre	350,000	2,000
Guatemala	Guatemala City	7,500,000	109,000
Guinea	Conakry	5,600,000	246,000
Guinea-Bissau	Bissau	800,000	36,000
Guyana	Georgetown	800,000	215,000
Haiti	Port-au-Prince	5,100,000	28,000
Honduras	Tegucigalpa	3,800,000	112,000
Hong Kong	Hong Kong	5,200,000	1,000
Hungary	Budapest	10,700,000	93,000
Iceland	Reykjavik	200,000	103,000
India	New Delhi	729,000,000	3,288,000
Indonesia	Jakarta	160,000,000	1,904,000
Iran	Tehrán	40,000,000	1,648,000
Iraq	Baghdad	13,500,000	435,000
Ireland	Dublin	3,400,000	70,000
Israel	Jerusalem	4,000,000	21,000
Italy	Rome	56,200,000	301,000
Ivory Coast	Abidjan	8,500,000	322,000
Jamaica	Kingston	2,200,000	11,000
Japan	Tokyo	117,600,000	372,000
Jordan	Amman	3,400,000	98,000
Kampuchea	Phnom Penh	7,100,000	181,000
Kenya	Nairobi	17,400,000	583,000
Kiribati	Tarawa	60,000	717
Korea, North	Pyongyang	18,700,000	121,000
Korea, South	Seoul	38,900,000	98,000
Kuwait	Kuwait	1,500,000	18,000

43

Country	Capital	Population	Area (sq km)
Laos	Vientiane	3,500,000	237,000
Lebanon	Beirut	2,700,000	10,000
Lesotho	Maseru	1,400,000	30,000
Liberia	Monrovia	1,900,000	111,000
Libya	Tripoli	3,100,000	1,760,000
Liechtenstein	Vaduz	30,000	160
Luxembourg	Luxembourg	400,000	3,000
Madagascar	Antananarivo	9,000,000	587,000
Malawi	Lilongwe	6,200,000	118,000
Malaysia	Kuala Lumpur	14,200,000	330,000
Maldives	Malé	200,000	300
Mali	Bamako	6,900,000	1,240,000
Malta	Valletta	400,000	300
Martinique	Fort-de-France	300,000	1,000
Mauritania	Nouakchott	1,600,000	1,031,000
Mauritius	Port Louis	1,000,000	2,000
Mexico	Mexico City	71,200,000	1,973,000
Monaco	Monaco	30,000	2
Mongolia	Ulaanbaatar	1,700,000	1,567,000
Morocco	Rabat	20,900,000	447,000
Mozambique	Maputo	12,500,000	783,000
Namibia	Windhoek	1,000,000	824,000
Nauru	Nauru	7,000	21
Nepal	Katmandu	15,000,000	141,000
Netherlands	Amsterdam	14,200,000	37,000
New Zealand	Wellington	3,300,000	269,000
Nicaragua	Managua	2,800,000	130,000
Niger	Niamey	5,700,000	1,267,000
Nigeria	Lagos	87,600,000	925,000
Norway	Oslo	4,100,000	324,000
Oman	Muscat	900,000	212,000
Pakistan	Islamabad	84,500,000	804,000
Panama	Panama City	1,900,000	77,000
Papua New Guinea	Port Moresby	3,100,000	462,000
Paraguay	Asunción	3,100,000	407,000
Peru	Lima	17,000,000	1,285,000
Philippines	Manila	49,600,000	300,000
Poland	Warsaw	35,900,000	313,000
Portugal	Lisbon	10,000,000	92,000
Puerto Rico	San Juan	3,700,000	9,000
Qatar	Doha	200,000	11,000
Reunion	Saint-Denis	500,000	3,000
Romania	Bucharest	22,500,000	238,000
Rwanda	Kigali	5,300,000	26,000
St Christopher-Nevis	Basseterre	50,000	300
St Lucia	Castries	100,000	600
St Vincent	Kingstown	100,000	389

Country	Capital	Population	Area (sq km)
San Marino	San Marino	20,000	61
São Tomé and Principe	São Tomé	100,000	1,000
Saudi Arabia	Riyadh	9,300,000	2,150,000
Senegal	Dakar	5,900,000	196,000
Seychelles	Victoria	60,000	440
Sierra Leone	Freetown	3,600,000	72,000
Singapore	Singapore	2,400,000	600
Solomon Islands	Honiara	200,000	28,000
Somalia	Mogadiscio	4,400,000	638,000
South Africa	Pretoria	29,500,000	1,221,000
Spain	Madrid	38,000,000	505,000
Sri Lanka	Colombo	15,000,000	66,000
Sudan	Khartoum	19,200,000	2,506,000
Surinam	Paramaribo	400,000	163,000
Swaziland	Mbabane	600,000	17,000
Sweden	Stockholm	8,300,000	450,000
Switzerland	Berne	6,500,000	41,000
Syria	Damascus	9,300,000	185,000
Taiwan	Taipei	18,300,000	36,000
Tanzania	Dodoma	19,100,000	945,000
Thailand	Bangkok	48,000,000	514,000
Togo	Lomé	2,700,000	56,000
Tonga	Nuku'alofa	100,000	800
Trinidad and Tobago	Port-of-Spain	1,200,000	5,000
Tunisia	Tunis	6,500,000	164,000
Turkey	Ankara	45,500,000	781,000
Tuvalu	Funafuti	10,000	26
Uganda	Kampala	13,000,000	236,000
USSR	Moscow	275,000,000	22,402,000
United Arab Emirates	Abu Dhabi	1,100,000	87,000
United Kingdom	London	56,000,000	244,000
USA	Washington DC	235,000,000	9,363,000
Uruguay	Montevideo	2,900,000	176,000
Vanuatu	Vila	100,000	15,000
Vatican City		1,000	0.4
Venezuela	Caracas	15,400,000	912,000
Vietnam	Hanoi	55,700,000	330,000
Virgin Islands	Road Town	10,000	100
Western Sahara	El Aaiún	120,000	267,800
Western Samoa	Apia	200,000	3,000
Yemen, North	Saná	7,300,000	195,000
Yemen, South	Aden	2,000,000	333,000
Yugoslavia	Belgrade	22,300,000	256,000
Zaire	Kinshasa	29,800,000	2,345,000
Zambia	Lusaka	5,800,000	753,000
Zimbabwe	Harare	7,200,000	391,000

Index

---

* Currency conversion chart (correct on July 16th, 1990)

	US $	Sing. $	NZ $	Aust. $	Can.$	£ Sterling
US $	1.0	1.82	1.68	1.28	1.16	0.56
Singapore $1	0.55	1.0	0.93	0.70	0.64	0.31
New Zealand $1	0.59	1.08	1.0	0.76	0.69	0.33
Australian $1	0.78	1.42	1.32	1.0	0.90	0.43
Canadian $1	0.87	1.57	1.46	1.11	1.0	0.48
£1 Sterling	1.80	3.27	3.03	2.30	2.08	1.0

48